INSPIRATIONAL LIVES

ANDY MURRAY

TENNIS CHAMPION

Clive Gifford

WAYLAND

First published in 2016 by Wayland

Copyright © Wayland 2016

Wayland is an imprint of
Hachette Children's Group
Part of Hodder & Stoughton
Carmelite House
50 Victoria Embankment
London EC4Y 0DZ

Editor: Nicola Edwards
Design: Basement68

A catalogue record for this title is
available from the British Library.

ISBN: 978 0 7502 9495 9
ebook ISBN: 978 0 7502 8540 7

FSC
www.fsc.org
MIX
Paper from
responsible sources
FSC® C104740

Printed in China

An Hachette UK company
www.hachette.co.uk
www.hachettechildrens.co.uk

Picture acknowledgements:
The author and publisher would like
to thank the following for allowing
their pictures to be reproduced in this
publication: Cover: Clive Brunskill/
Getty Images; p4 Getty Images; p5 Clive
Brunskill/Getty Images; p6 Andrew
Parsons/PA Archive/Press Association
Images); p7 Andrew Milligan/PA Wire; p8
Andrew Milligan/PA Wire; p9 Fernando
Bustamante/AP/Press Association
Images; p10 Craig Prentis/Getty Images;
p11 Clive Brunskill/Getty Images; p12
Patrick Straub/Getty Images; p13 Ryan
Pierse/Getty Images; p14 Tony Avelar/
AP/Press Association Images; p15 Don
Emmert/AFP/Getty Images; p16 Clive
Brunskill/Getty Images; p17 Carl De
Souza/AFP/Getty Images; p18 Lionel
Cironneau/AP/Press Association
Images; p19 Jeff Moore/Jeff Moore/
Empics Entertainment; p20 lev radin /
Shutterstock.com; p21 Julian Finney/
Getty Images; p22 Paul Gilham/Getty
Images; p23 Gouhier-Guibbaud-JMP/
ABACA/Press Association Images; p24
lev radin / Shutterstock.com; p25 Corinne
Dubreuil /ABACA/Press Association
Images; p26 Featureflash / Shutterstock.
com; p27 Corinne Dubreuil /ABACA/Press
Association Images; p28 Ian MacNicol/
AFP/GettyImages; p29 Jonathan Brady/
PA Wire

Contents

Winning Wimbledon

Sunday 7th July 2013 and Andy Murray walked out onto Wimbledon's centre court for the final of the men's singles. The pressure was really on. No British man had won this tournament since Fred Perry triumphed in 1936 and none had even reached the final since Bunny Austin in 1938. Andy Murray knew the history. He had made his first visit to Wimbledon with the Dunblane Sports Club as a seven-year-old fan, and had first appeared in the men's competition as an 18-year-old in 2005.

Andy had cruised through the early rounds of the 2013 tournament without dropping a **set** until he reached the quarter-finals. Quickly, he found himself two sets down to Fernando Verdasco of Spain and in real peril of being knocked out as so many other British hopefuls had been over the years.

But he rallied to win that match in five sets and defeat Poland's Jerzy Janowicz Jr. in the semi-finals. In the final Andy faced the player ranked as number one in the world: Novak Djokovic.

WOW!

Andy's Wimbledon win inspired a staggering 120,000 tweets on Twitter in a single minute during the climax of his match against Djokovic.

*Andy Murray hits a **backhand** shot on his way to victory in the Wimbledon men's singles final in 2013.*

Andy's previous matches with Djokovic had often been tough, long battles. Several of their matches had lasted almost five hours so it was no surprise that the very first game took five minutes and the first set one minute short of an hour. Andy got off to a winning start and when he won the second set as well, 7-5, many of the 15,000 crammed into Centre Court started to really believe he could triumph.

Djokovic, though, had other ideas and the brilliant Serbian unleashed many astonishing winning shots. The pair battled hard through some incredibly long and punishing **rallies**. Andy said after the match, "I don't expect to ever have a harder game. The points were unbelievably hard but it was something I wasn't going to let go." He certainly needed all of his nerve to hold his **serve** and win the third set 6-4. The Centre Court crowd erupted. Andy Murray had done it!

Andy proudly holds his Wimbledon trophy after beating Novak Djokovic in the final.

INSPIRATION

Murray dedicated his Wimbledon triumph to his *coach*, Ivan Lendl. Andy said, "He believed in me when a lot of people didn't... I'm just happy I managed to do it for him."

Growing up in Dunblane

Andrew Barron Murray was born on the 15th of May, 1987. He and his older brother, Jamie, were brought up in the small Scottish town of Dunblane by their parents, Judy and William. A tennis coach, Judy had been a professional tennis player, winning 64 Scottish ladies and girls titles. Her lively young sons enjoyed the fun activities and games she organised for them.

Games in the Murray household included kicking and hitting sponge balls around the house, and hitting a Swingball (a tennis ball on a pole that could be hit back and forth) in the garden.

Andy recalls how poor he was at first, saying, "I had bad concentration, bad co-ordination and a temper. It was not a good combination." Andy's competiveness even extended to playing board games – he'd get really upset and sometimes topple the board over if he didn't win.

Aged 17, Andy is photographed with his mother and father at Wimbledon in 2004.

INSPIRATION

"I can't remember the last time I was in an argument with her. My mum's the one person who gets me, who understands me really well." – Andy about his mother, Judy.

Andy enjoyed the tennis games with his family, and as he grew older, his abilities improved. The Dunblane Sports Club was just 200m from their home and it wasn't long before Andy could be found there. He would hit balls and compete against his brother and their friends from school, using his first-ever tennis racquet with its purple metal frame, which he has kept to this day. In fact such was Andy's passion for tennis and other sports, that he didn't like lessons much and couldn't wait to get out of the classroom and play.

In March 1996 when Andy was eight, the small Scottish town was suddenly in the news after a terrible tragedy struck his school. Sixteen children and a teacher were killed in a horrific attack carried out by a lone gunman. Andy and Jamie were both in school that day. Andy has rarely spoken in public about the subject, although in a 2013 TV documentary he told his interviewer, "You have no idea how tough something like that is," and said how he was glad in his career, "to do something the town is proud of".

TOP TIP

Andy's parents always encouraged Andy and Jamie to try out different sports and didn't force them into playing tennis. As Andy noted in an interview, "Mum and Dad always said to me, 'As long as you're happy, that's the most important thing.'"

On a visit to his home town of Dunblane in 2012, local children present Andy with congratulations cards to celebrate his wins at the London Olympics and the US Open.

Brother v brother

Andy and Jamie's parents split up when Andy was ten years old. Judy Murray moved out of the family home but still saw the boys regularly while William brought them up. The brothers were close even though they battled hard. Whether it was football, tennis or wrestling, much of Andy's sporting energies before he was a teenager were taken up competing against his brother.

Taller, stronger and fifteen months older than Andy, Jamie was a tough opponent, whether the boys were hitting balls over the net or grappling with each other in mock wrestling bouts. The brothers made champions belts like those the World Wrestling Federation (WWF) stars wore, but Jamie only let Andy win the women's belts!

Andy and Jamie's grandfather, Roy Erskine, had been a professional footballer and Andy grew up supporting Roy's former Scottish club, Hibernians, as well as playing for a local team, Gairdoch United. He was good enough as a striker to be scouted by Glasgow Rangers, one of the biggest sides in Scotland, as he reached his teens, but choose tennis over football.

Will Murray with a framed photo of his sons, Andy and Jamie, not yet in their teens but both already tennis-mad.

INSPIRATION

"I had my brother to play with which really helped me and he was always better than me growing up, so that was someone for me to look up to and then to try and beat and compete with," – Andy on his brother, Jamie.

Both brothers took part in junior tennis tournaments at a young age and Andy was only eight when he won his very first, the Solihull Under-10s event in Birmingham. He received £50 prize money, and quickly spent it on computer games! The brothers were sometimes drawn against each other in tournaments and early on, Jamie usually won. However, when Andy was 10, he beat his older brother in the final of the Solihull tournament and goaded him about it on the long drive home to Scotland. Jamie finally lost his temper and hit Andy's hand so hard that, to this day, Andy has not been able to grow a full nail on one of his fingers.

Despite the incident, the brothers remained close and played doubles matches together for many years. In his 2009 **autobiography**, *Coming Of Age*, Andy maintained that he gets more nervous watching his big brother playing an important match than playing his own games. Two years later, Jamie and Andy teamed up again to win the men's doubles at the Japanese Open Championships.

Jamie (left) and Andy celebrate after reaching the final of the 2010 Valencia Open men's doubles competition. The brothers would win the final against Max Mirnyi and Mahesh Bhupathi.

WOW!

Jamie became a grand slam champion five years before his brother when he and Jelena Jankovic won the 2007 Wimbledon mixed doubles title.

Rising through the ranks

Andy enjoyed plenty of success in his early career. Aged just 12, he won the highly-prized Junior Orange Bowl Championship in Florida, USA. But his ferocious desre to win sometimes caused him problems, such as when he was dismissed from the Scottish Junior Championships, also when he was 12, for losing his temper and throwing his racquet while on court.

When Andy's brother Jamie was 12, he left home for a tennis boarding school in Cambridge run by the Lawn Tennis Association (LTA). Jamie hated it and came back seven months later having fallen out of love with tennis. Andy knew he didn't want to have the same unhappy experience. Even so, as he grew older, finding players of his standard to train and practise with was starting to prove a problem. He feared he was falling behind rivals of his age in other countries. At tournaments he found out that many of them were training in well-organised camps and academies in Europe.

Andy in action at the 1999 National Junior Championships in Nottingham, where he won the Under-14s event.

TOP TIP

As Andy learned to control his teenage temper more, he found he could breathe better and concentrate on his tactics in a match. He still keeps the passion in his play but now tries to put mistakes behind him so they don't cloud his thoughts.

When Andy was 15, his family made a big decision. They raised £40,000 so that Andy could attend the Sanchez-Casal Tennis Academy in Barcelona, Spain, for 18 months. There, the better climate and excellent facilities, which included 29 courts, along with being able to play regularly against tough opponents allowed Andy to work really hard on his game.

Andy grew up a lot in those 18 months away from home. Despite the hard work, tough training and occasional homesickness, he enjoyed mixing with talented players and being independent. He made lasting friendships with several of the boys he met there, including Dani Vallverdu from Venezuela, who would later become part of Andy's team as a practice partner.

Murray's tennis improved during his time in Spain. As he got older in the juniors he won some big events, including the Canadian Junior Open and, in 2004, the Junior US Open, becoming the first ever British winner of that event. The year before, Andy had suffered his first major injury scare with a painful knee. It turned out that he had a bipartite patella on his right knee – his kneecap was made of two separate bones instead of one.

Andy shakes hands with Sergiy Stakhovsky from Ukraine after winning the 2004 Junior US Open singles final. Andy and Jamie also reached the semi-finals of the doubles competition.

WOW!

Andy won the 2004 BBC Young Sports Personality of the Year award. He nearly didn't make it to the TV show in time, though, because he got stuck in a locked bathroom for 30 minutes!

11

Turning pro

Andy stepped up from the juniors to join the Association of Tennis Professionals (**ATP**) tour in April 2005. He was only 17 years old and had a lowly world ranking of 407. Many of the bigger tournaments only offer places to the top 32 or 64 players in the world, so Andy had to play lesser tournaments on the Challengers and Futures circuits and hope to rise through the rankings.

Andy's first ATP match was in a tournament in Barcelona against Jan Hernych who was ranked 67th in the world. Andy won the first set, but failed to control the match and missed more than a dozen chances to break his opponent's serve. He lost two sets to one and was furious with his performance. Over the next few months, Andy played in adult tournaments but also some juniors events such as the French Open in June where he reached the semi-finals.

*Andy comes into the net to hit a **volley,** on his way to beating Tim Henman by two sets to one at the Davidoff Swiss Indoors tournament in 2005.*

INSPIRATION

"Tim was a great player. He was also my friend, he was my mentor and I looked up to him...he was so generous with me with his time and advice."
— Andy on Tim Henman who helped Andy adjust to the rigours of the ATP tour in his early years on it.

As a young British player, Andy was given 'wild card' invitations to appear at two major ATP tournaments in London. The first was at The Queen's Club where he won his first ever ATP tour matches against Santiago Ventura and Taylor Dent. The second was at Wimbledon where he also won two matches and got his first taste of the intense **media** and fan interest in any successful British players.

Andy holds his runners up plate alongside Roger Federer after the 2005 Thailand Open final. Andy lost the match 6-3, 7-5.

Andy's career was well on the rise, and winning two tournaments on the Futures tour in 2005 helped his world ranking rise. So did an amazing run at the Thailand Open where he defeated a succession of higher-ranked players to reach his first ATP tournament final. Facing him over the net was the imposing figure of Roger Federer. Andy had only ever played him in computer games and was a little overawed. He lost easily but was excited by and gained confidence from the experience. At the end of the season, he found himself just inside the world's top 100. It was a fantastic start to his adult career, but he knew a long road and much hard work ahead lay ahead.

WOW!

Murray was so nervous when he met and practised with his boyhood idol, Andre Agassi at The Queen's Club in 2006, that his hands got sweaty and he forgot his water bottle!

Breaking into the elite

In 2006, Andy travelled to the SAP Open in San Jose, in the United States. Previous winners of the event included tennis greats such as Pete Sampras, Andre Agassi and John McEnroe. Andy not only managed to reach the final, beating the world number three player, Andy Roddick along the way, but also beat Lleyton Hewitt in the final itself. Andy had won his first ATP tour title.

Andy ended the 2006 season ranked as the world number 17, and the following year edged into the top ten ranked players in the world, but it wasn't a smooth path to the top. He had to contend with some tough defeats and the media criticism that followed them. At the Beijing Olympics, for example, he was knocked out in the first round by Yen-Hsun Lu of Taiwan, a player ranked some 70 places below him.

Andy raises the glass trophy after winning the 2006 SAP Open, his first ATP tour title.

INSPIRATION

The venue for Andy's first ATP tournament title was an ice hockey arena. It featured a sign that Andy has taken to heart as good advice: "Hard work beats talent when talent doesn't work hard."

As Andy was still growing, his body sometimes struggled with the demands of tennis. He suffered from muscle cramps, for example, and on occasion had to pull out of matches with niggling injuries. Worse was to come when Andy found himself spending his 20th birthday in hospital after tearing a tendon in his wrist during a tournament in Germany. He had to sit out three frustrating months right in the middle of the season until it healed.

During the 2008 season, though, Andy really made his mark. He won five ATP tournaments in Qatar, France, the United States, Russia and Spain as well as reaching his first ever grand slam final. The four biggest tournaments in the world (the Australian Open, the French Open, Wimbledon and the US Open) are known as grand slams and every professional tennis player dreams of winning one. Andy had a fabulous run in the US Open, the highlight being an astonishing win over the world number one, Rafael Nadal, as he became the first British player to reach a grand slam final since Greg Rusedski in 1997.

WOW!

In 2009, Andy became the first British winner of the Queen's tournament in London for 71 years.

Andy is stunned and delighted to beat the number one seed, Rafael Nadal (right), in four sets to reach the final of the 2008 US Open.

Team Murray

Andy was coached through much of his early career by Leon Smith and the staff at the academy in Spain. Once he began competing on the ATP tour, he started working with different tennis coaches including Mark Petchey, Brad Gilbert, Miles Maclagan and from the end of 2011, Ivan Lendl. Andy's coach is just one member of a close-knit team he has built up around him to attend training and travel with him to tournaments.

Professional tennis places enormous stresses on the body and Andy works incredibly hard on his overall fitness. Top players need to be able to sprint hard, react and change direction sharply and be capable of performing at their very best for three, four or more hours of a long, tough match.

Andy climbs up part of Centre Court to celebrate his 2013 Wimbledon success with his coaching team, including Ivan Lendl (in sunglasses) and Dani Vallverdu (right of Lendl).

INSPIRATION

"Staying more controlled mentally stemmed from me taking my fitness more seriously. When you're doing track work, sprints and so on, it's pretty painful, but that does make you feel better prepared and therefore mentally stronger when you're going into a match." – Andy on his fitness regime.

Under the close eye of his fitness coach, Jez Green, Andy performs gruelling training exercises, such as running twenty 100m sprints in a row, one every minute. He also works hard to improve his **stamina** and add strength to his muscles so that he can hit the ball with more power and perform better for longer during competition.

During a tournament, players who recover the best from their previous match give themselves the best chance in their next. Andy employs masseuses to keep his leg, arm and back muscles loose and relaxed after exercise and will often take a freezing cold ice bath to help recovery. He also practises Bikram yoga, which is performed in a very hot room, to help improve his body's flexibility and reduce the chance of injuries.

Expert **nutritionists** plan Andy's diet to make sure he gets the right amount of energy and nutrients to keep his body in peak condition. After getting drunk once as a teenager in Spain and not enjoying the experience, Andy avoids drinking alcohol. He tries to eat something within 30 minutes of finishing a match to help his body recover.

Andy works on his sprinting strength at The Queen's Club in London under the eye of his fitness trainer, Jez Green (left).

WOW!

Sushi is high in protein and low in fat. Andy can eat more than 40 pieces of sushi in a single meal!

Joining the 'big three'

By 2009, Andy was a top-ten ranked player and often appeared in the later stages of major tournaments. He reached the semi-finals of Wimbledon for the first time that year and elite players now considered him to be a very tough opponent.

Andy won six tournaments in 2009 and five in 2011. He collected over US$ 9 million in prize money in those two seasons alone, yet a precious grand slam title continued to be just beyond him. His path to glory always seemed to be blocked by one of the three of the greatest players the tennis world has seen: Roger Federer, Rafael Nadal and Novak Djokovic. Any one of these players might have dominated another era of tennis, but instead they were competing against each other – and Andy – at the same tournaments.

At the 2009 Monte Carlo Tennis Masters, played on clay courts, Andy suffered his seventh defeat in nine matches against Rafael Nadal.

TOP TIP

For Andy, a good serve starts with the ball toss and the secret is to stay loose and make it smooth and consistent. He says: "For sure technique is more important than muscles when you're still developing your game."

Between late 2008 and early 2012, for example, Andy lost nine tournament finals and only one of those defeats was not to one of the 'big three'. He also lost to Rafael Nadal four times in grand slam semi-finals. He trained incredibly hard and felt he was getting closer to the big three. He managed to beat both Federer and Nadal twice in 2010 and Nadal twice in 2011, but kept on losing at the semi-final or final stage of grand slam tournaments.

Andy was introduced to Ivan Lendl in late 2011. The former Czech player had won eight grand slam tournaments and an incredible 94 ATP events overall so was a proven winner. Lendl's experience showed Andy how he could make tiny but crucial improvements to the way he played. As Andy said in the summer of 2012, "There's not been one radical change. A lot of it is minor details. But if you pick ten small things to work on and change, that can turn into a big difference."

WOW!

By July 2013, Andy had hit 3,709 aces (when his serve was unplayable by his opponent) during his ATP career.

During practice before the 2013 Wimbledon final, Andy hits a double-handed backhand shot, watched by his coach, Ivan Lendl.

A day in the life of Andy Murray

Andy's life varies greatly. Days in training or at a tournament are quite different from the time he spends on the road travelling between tournaments, handling business commitments or dealing with the world's media.

As an elite professional tennis player, Andy is on the ATP Tour which runs from the start of January into November. It's a long season and top pros like Andy clock up tens of thousands of kilometres on planes as they criss-cross the globe between training bases, seeing family and playing around 20 tournaments a season on all continents. In 2012, for example, Andy played tournaments in Australia, China, Canada, the United States, Europe, Dubai and Japan among other places.

Andy answers questions from the media during the 2012 US Open. Players are expected to appear at many press conferences throughout a tournament.

WOW!

In 2013, Andy was awarded an OBE for his service to tennis. At a ceremony at Buckingham Palace in London he received his award from the Duke of Cambridge.

Andy has always said that the competition and winning is what motivates him to play tennis. Money may not spur him on, but becoming one of the world's best players certainly brings financial rewards. Andy is managed by Simon Fuller who also manages David Beckham, and has signed deals with a number of **sponsors** including the Royal Bank of Scotland, sportswear company, Adidas and the makers of his tennis racquets, Head. He may spend parts of some days filming adverts or taking part in promotions for his sponsors.

Dealing regularly with the media has become a fact of life for Andy as he rose through the rankings. Early on, he had several difficult moments when his deadpan sense of humour was reported as him being serious and caused offence. In 2006, for example, after joking with Tim Henman who mocked the Scottish football team not reaching the FIFA World Cup, Andy said he would support any team that played against England. It was a joke, but many people took his words seriously and believed he was anti-English for many years.

As a result of such incidents, Andy can be wary of the media but not of tennis fans. He remembers how he was one and how disappointed he was as a child when he couldn't get Andre Agassi's signature at a tournament. As a result, he tries to sign as many autographs as possible.

WOW!

In 2012, Andy signed a deal to appear in adverts and as an ambassador for luxury watchmakers, RADO. Andy is due to receive around £9 million from this sponsorship deal.

Andy is surrounded by fans, all after his autograph, after he has completed a match at the BNP Paribas Tennis Classic in 2013.

Highs and lows: the 2012 season

With Ivan Lendl as part of his team, Andy entered the 2012 season in good heart, especially after winning the first tournament of the year, the Brisbane Open. Andy now had 22 ATP titles but thirsted for a grand slam tournament victory.

He only lost one of the 16 sets he played at the Australian Open to reach the semi-finals. But there he faced the defending champion, Novak Djokovic. The pair slugged it out, trading powerful **forehand** passes with delicate **drop shots** and **lobs** in almost five hours of compelling tennis. After Djokovic won the first set, Andy roared back to take the next two, but his opponent took the fourth and fifth sets and won the match. It was a bitter disappointment.

Andy put this defeat behind him and reached the quarter-finals or better of five further tournaments before playing at Wimbledon. Expectations from the home crowd rose as he defeated Nikolai Davydenko, David Ferrer, Ivo Karlovi and Jo-Wilfred Tsonga and made it into his first ever Wimbledon final. However, his opponent in the final, Roger Federer, was to prove too strong for him. Andy called it the hardest loss of his career, breaking down in tears during his runners-up speech.

Andy's disappointment is clear as he walks to the net after losing to Roger Federer in the 2012 Wimbledon final.

Andy's next competitive tennis match, three weeks later, was also against a Swiss player at Wimbledon but this time the player was Stanislas Wawrinka and the match was the first round of the London 2012 Olympics. Andy loved being part of Team GB at the games and paired up with Laura Robson in the mixed doubles as well as competing in the men's singles. He reached the final of both competitions losing in the mixed doubles but only after pulling out one of his finest ever performances to beat Roger Federer convincingly in three sets: 6-2, 6-1, 6-4. Andy was the Olympic men's singles champion. "It's the biggest win of my life," he said.

WOW!

Andy couldn't sleep for many nights after winning Olympic gold, the first by a British male player since 1908.

Andy jumps for joy as he beats Roger Federer at the 2012 Olympic Games. He was only the seventh man to win two tennis medals at a single Olympics.

INSPIRATION

"Being around the Olympics and seeing how the nation came together, from the public to the athletes to the press ...It's been so much fun and I'm just happy I was able to contribute towards it."
– Andy after winning Olympic gold.

23

A first grand slam

There was little time for Andy to bask in the glory of being Olympic champion. Within days, he had flown across the Atlantic to Toronto in Canada to take part in the Rogers Cup tournament, a traditional warm-up event for the US Open, which takes place later in August.

Andy started well in the Rogers Cup, beating Flavio Cipolla comfortably, but felt pain in his knee during his next match and pulled out of the tournament. He moved on to the Western and Southern Open in the United States but lost in his first match to American Sam Querry.

Some fans were doubtful of Andy's chances at the US Open, but the tournament started well for him. He won two matches in straight sets and then another in a close fight with world number 31 Feliciano Lopez, winning all three sets on tiebreaks. He endured a tough semi-final against Tomáš Berdych, losing the first set before powering through in very windy conditions.

Andy serves against Tomáš Berdych during their 2012 US Open semi-final. The match lasted almost four hours.

WOW!

Murray relaxed before the US Open final by watching The *Wedding Crashers* movie and playing Scrabble.

After a single rest day, Andy entered the final against Novak Djokovic aware that he had only won one of 13 sets in grand slam finals. The first set was a monster, lasting 87 minutes and featuring a 24-minute-long tiebreak, the longest in any final, which Andy eventually won 12 points to 10. Murray raced into a 4-0 lead in the second set, but Djokovic fought back to 5-5 only to lose the set. Murray was now just one set away from glory, but the Serbian played some astonishing tennis to level the match at two sets all.

It took all of Andy's reserves to lift himself for one final set, but he managed it, breaking his opponent's serve three times in the final set. After an epic 4 hour, 54 minute match, the longest US Open Final since 1987, Andy had triumphed: 7–6, 7–5, 2–6, 3–6, 6–2. "It is what I have been working towards for the last ten years of my life," he said afterwards. "It means the world to me."

INSPIRATION

Murray took a toilet break after the fourth set in the final and stared at the mirror trying to regain his focus. He revealed later that he told himself, "For one set, just give it everything you've got. You don't want to come off this court with any regrets."

Andy holds the US Open trophy aloft watched by the opponent he defeated in the final, Novak Djokovic.

Off the court

Tennis, training and travel take up much of Andy's time but away from the tennis circuit, he still gets time to do other things that he enjoys including spending time with his wife, Kim Sears, watching movies and DVD box sets such as *Sherlock*, and listening to music (his favourite artistes include Black Eyed Peas, 50 Cent and Eminem).

Andy spent his first ever tournament winnings on computer games and continues to be an ardent gamer. His Playstation games console has his name on the front and goes with him on tour where he has played football onscreen against other players, particularly Rafael Nadal. Andy also amused journalists when he reported that he had won Wimbledon many times...on his Playstation tennis game.

Andy and Kim Sears arrive in London for an event held as part of London Fashion Week in 2012. Andy was nominated for a Scottish fashion award the following year.

WOW!

Andy and Kim have two border terrier dogs, Rusty and Maggie May. The latter has her own Twitter account with more than 28,000 followers!

Andy is a massive sports fan both as a spectator and participant and prefers holidays where he can stay active. He is keen on golf and motorsports although he quickly sold the Ferrari F430 sportscar he bought in 2009 as he admitted he "felt like an idiot" driving it. He prefers go-karting on tracks and has his own racing helmet and shoes. He admires boxing greatly and has trained with British boxer, Amir Khan. He likens boxing to tennis saying in his autobiography, "It's all about performing well in front of a big crowd with one man out to stop you."

Although he does not attend many celebrity events Andy enjoys being around people, whether it is his Team Murray pals, friends like Ross Hutchins (see panel) or his family. Andy was best man at his brother Jamie's wedding in 2010 and two years later bought the country house near Dunblane which hosted the occasion. In 2015, Andy and Kim held their own wedding reception there too. He likes sightseeing but doesn't get much chance in and around tournaments but he often brings back one souvenir from tournaments: the towels the players are given!

Andy chases down the ball during a 2011 charity football match for earthquake victims in Japan. Andy scored for his team in a 4-2 loss to US soccer side, Fort Lauderdale Strikers.

INSPIRATION

Watching his close friend, Ross Hutchins, battle cancer successfully has inspired Andy to put many of his own problems into perspective. Hutchins stated in interviews that Andy was "absolutely unbelievable and so supportive with me the whole way."

The impact of Andy Murray

Andy Murray is Britain's most successful tennis player for over 70 years. He has already won two grand slams, more than 25 top-flight tournaments and is ranked in the top three in the world – a stunning achievement especially in an era of intense competition. With plenty of seasons ahead of him, he could go on to win many more tournaments and become world number one.

Murray is a proud Scotsman who was thrilled by how his hometown of Dunblane got behind him during his journey to glory, but he is also just as proud to be British. After his 2013 grand slam triumph he said, "That win was for myself but I also understand how much everyone else wanted to see a British winner at Wimbledon. I hope you guys enjoyed it."

Andy shows his Olympic medals to delighted fans in Dunblane during a visit in 2012. Andy knows he is a role model for young people and hopes his example can inspire them.

TOP TIP

"To succeed you need a mindset to work hard, which is what two little guys from Dunblane have done. How many people in British tennis have done what Andy has done?"
– William Murray, Andy's Dad.

Andy's success makes him one of the biggest sports stars in the UK. His 2013 Wimbledon triumph was watched at its peak by 17.3 million TV viewers in Britain, the most of any sporting event that year. He has already inspired thousands of boys and girls to take up tennis. In Dunblane, for example, six times as many children are now playing tennis than previously. Andy is keen to see many more children given the opportunity to play tennis and has supported a number of different schemes to get kids into tennis and other sports.

Off the court, Andy doesn't go out of his way to gain publicity unless it is for a good cause. He was a founding member of the Malaria No More UK Leadership Council and helped launch the charity in 2009 with David Beckham. He has also appeared in videos for Sports Relief and appeared at the Rally Against Cancer tennis event in London in 2013 where he played in a doubles match with Tim Henman against his coach, Ivan Lendl. The event raised almost £200,000 for the Royal Marsden Cancer Charity.

Andy and close friend, Ross Hutchins share a joke during the Rally Against Cancer charity doubles match at The Queen's Club in London in 2013.

WOW!

Andy donated all his prize money for winning the AEGON Championships in 2013, a cool £73,000, to the Royal Marsden Cancer Charity.

Have you got what it takes to be a tennis champion?

1) Do you enjoy playing tennis and do you play regularly?
a) Yes, I love tennis. I play as often as I can and often beat my friends.
b) I quite enjoy playing and play several games a year, mainly in the summer.
c) I only play now and then when friends really want to as it's not my favourite pastime.

2) Are you fit and into fast-moving ball sports like basketball, netball, football, squash or hockey?
a) Yes, I really enjoy sports with plenty of action and skill and play them all the time.
b) I like some sports but am puffed out after playing for a short while.
c) I'm not very fit or all that interested in playing other sports.

3) Are you good at taking advice to improve a skill, such as your tennis strokes?
a) Yes, I think so. I listen carefully and then practise what I've learnt as much as possible.
b) I'd take the advice and might practise if I had time but not always.
c) Not really. I'm happy with how I play and don't want to change anything.

4) How do you react when you lose a tennis match or some other individual sport?
a) I hate losing, but vow to make up for it next time.
b) I get angry and upset and don't play that game or sport for a long time afterwards.
c) I don't mind losing or winning. Competing against others doesn't really interest me.

5) If you found yourself playing tennis against an opponent who was bigger and older than you, how would you react?
a) I would be even more determined to beat them and would really play hard.
b) I'd protest that it was unfair but would probably play even though I didn't think I had a chance.
c) I wouldn't play.

6) Would you be prepared to give up lots of your social life to practise and train hard many times per week?
a) Yes. I understand I'd have to make sacrifices to become a good player.
b) I don't mind some practice, but want to have plenty of time with my friends.
c) No chance! Going out with my friends is what matters most to me.

RESULTS

Mostly As: It sounds like you may have the right attitude and possibly, the ability, to go far in tennis. Why not visit your local tennis club and ask about training and games for juniors.

Mostly Bs: It sounds as if you like tennis but are more into casual games than competing at a serious level. Keep enjoying your tennis but think about getting some coaching to improve or organising a mini-tournament among your friends.

Mostly Cs: It doesn't sound as if taking up tennis seriously is for you...at least, not at the moment. You might still want to play with friends. It can be lots of fun.

Glossary

ace A serve that the opposing player is unable to get their racket to and return.

ATP Short for the Association of Tennis Professionals, a body which organises the men's professional tennis circuit.

autobiography A book about a person's life written by that person or with some assistance from a professional writer.

backhand A tennis shot hit from the side of the body opposite the racket-holding arm.

coach A training or fitness advisor.

drop shots Delicate tennis shots that just clear the net and fall short in the opponent's court.

forehand A tennis shot hit from the same side of the body as the arm and hand that holds the racket.

grand slam A term used to describe the four biggest tournaments in professional tennis: the Australian Open, the French Open, Wimbledon and the US Open.

lobs Tennis hots that are hit high into the air so that they travel above an opponent's head and land behind them.

media Ways of communicating, for example through TV, radio, newspapers or websites.

mixed doubles Tennis matches featuring a boy and girl or man and woman on each two-person team.

nutritionist A health professional who plans diets for people and advises them on how to eat healthily.

OBE Short for 'Officer of the Most Excellent Order of the British Empire', an award given to recognise exceptional achievement or service.

rallies Exchanges of tennis shots between the players across a series of points.

role model Someone who is successful in sport or some other field. The way they behave is often copied by others, especially young people.

serve How a point in tennis begins when players hit the ball powerfully above their head into their opponent's half of the court. You 'hold your serve' if you win the game when it is your turn to serve. If your opponent wins the game when you are serving, this is known as a 'break of serve'.

set A group of games in tennis. A set is won if a player reaches six or more winning games in the set and is two games ahead of his or her opponent or if a player wins a tie break (the system used in many competitions to decide a set after the scores are tied at six games each).

sponsors Companies that pay money to someone in return for advertising their products, for example by wearing clothing with a company's logo.

stamina The ability to maintain physical effort over an extended period of time.

sushi Japanese dishes of cold cooked rice flavoured with vinegar and combined with other foods such as fish and vegetables.

volley A tennis shot in which the player hits the ball before it bounces on the ground.

Index